W9-CMZ-005

Built for Speed

The World's Fastest Dragsters

by Glen and Karen Bledsoe

Consultants:
The staff of the
Museum of Drag Racing
Ocala, Florida

CAPSTONE
HIGH-INTEREST
BOOKS

an imprint of Capstone Press
Mankato, Minnesota

Capstone High-Interest Books are published by Capstone Press
151 Good Counsel Drive, P.O. Box 669, Mankato, Minnesota 56002
http://www.capstone-press.com

Library of Congress Cataloging-in-Publication Data
Bledsoe, Glen.
  The world's fastest dragsters/by Glen and Karen Bledsoe.
  p. cm.—(Built for speed)
  Summary: Examines the excitement, history, regulations, types of cars, and notable drivers of drag racing.
  Includes bibliographical references and index.
  ISBN 0-7368-1500-7 (hardcover)
  1. Dragsters—Juvenile literature. [1. Drag racing. 2. Automobiles, Racing.]
I. Bledsoe, Karen E. II. Title. III. Built for speed (Mankato, Minn.) IV. Series.
TL236.2 .B58 2003
796.72—dc21   2002012616

Editorial Credits
Matt Doeden, editor; Karen Risch, product planning editor; Timothy Halldin,
    series designer; Patrick Dentinger, book designer; Jo Miller, photo researcher

Photo Credits
Auto Imagery, Inc., 36
Corbis/AFP, 19
Getty Images/Jamie Squire, cover, 9, 25; Jon Ferrey, 13, 31; Ken Levine, 16;
    Darren England, 39; Mike Powell, 44
Photo courtesy of Steve Embling/DragRaceCanada.com, 40
Photo Network/Mark Sherman, 26, 35
SportsChrome-USA, 10; Rob Tringali Jr., 4, 7, 14, 20, 22–23, 28, 32
www.ronkimballstock.com, 47

1 2 3 4 5 6 08 07 06 05 04 03

Table of Contents

Rubber-Seal
PRODUCTS
Rubber-Seal
PRODUCTS
Autolite
SIMPSON
XRP
VENOLIA

Chapter 1

Dragsters

Two long, narrow cars sit side by side on a concrete slab. Their engines roar as the drivers get ready for a drag race. A green starting light flashes to signal the beginning of the race. The cars' wheels spin and their tires screech as the drivers accelerate as quickly as they can.

In less than 1 second, the dragsters reach a speed of more than 100 miles (160 kilometers) per hour. They are traveling more than 300 miles (480 kilometers) per hour as they cross the finish line. Parachutes open behind the dragsters to help them slow down. The race is over in less than 5 seconds.

Dragsters use powerful engines to reach speeds of more than 300 miles (480 kilometers) per hour.

Drag Racing

Drag races are the world's fastest and shortest races. They are held on short, straight strips of paved asphalt. Many drag strips have a slab of concrete, called a launch pad, at the starting line. Most drag races are 1,320 feet (402 meters) long. This distance is about one-fourth of a mile. Some drag races are only 660 feet (201 meters) long, or about one-eighth of a mile. Dragsters can complete these short races in a few seconds.

Two cars compete in a drag race. Each race is called an elimination. Dragsters begin at a standing stop. Their engines are running, but the cars are standing still. A light pole, called a Christmas tree, counts down the seconds before the start of the race.

Drag racing competitions are tournaments. The winner of each elimination moves on to the next round. Two drivers reach the final race. The winner of this race earns the title "top eliminator."

A light pole, called a Christmas tree, counts down the seconds before the start of the race.

Drag Racing History

Drag racing began in southern California in the 1930s. Some drivers there liked to work on their cars to make them fast. They called their cars "hot rods." Drivers often challenged each other to see whose hot rod was faster. They held some of these races on the main street of their town, which was often called the "main drag." Some people believe the name "drag racing" came from this term.

Racing in the streets was against the law. Police often arrested drivers who took part in these races. Racing was also dangerous to drivers and to people on the streets.

In the late 1940s, a police officer named Bud Coons wanted people to race legally and safely. He set up classes where he taught drivers how to take care of their cars. He also taught drivers to race their cars on tracks built just for racing. Illegal drag racing declined as a result of Coons' efforts.

A racing fan named Wally Parks was also concerned about illegal racing. He started an

The NHRA holds many of the biggest drag racing events in the United States.

organization called the National Hot Rod Association (NHRA). This group held legal drag races. The NHRA also helped set safety rules for the sport. For example, drivers had to wear helmets. Cars had to have strong metal roll bars that prevent the top of a car from being crushed in a roll.

Drivers enjoyed the organized drag races. They continued to improve car designs. They built cars with lighter frames. They added wider tires that gripped the track better. They moved the engines to the rear of the cars to protect drivers from engine fires. All of these changes made the cars faster and safer.

Drag Racing Today

Today, almost any kind of vehicle can be used in drag racing. The NHRA holds races for more than 200 vehicle classes, including cars, trucks, and motorcycles. The most popular types of dragsters are top fuel dragsters, pro stock dragsters, and nitro funny cars.

Modern dragsters are built just for racing. Designers give dragsters a streamlined design that reduces air resistance. These designs have mainly angled surfaces. Flat areas on cars cause air resistance.

Most dragsters have an airfoil attached to the rear. Air travels over this wing-shaped piece and pushes the rear of a dragster down.

Dragsters have a streamlined design that reduces air resistance.

This force is called "downforce." Downforce helps press the rear tires against the track to give them better grip.

Safety is a big concern for drivers and race organizers. All dragsters must include a safety cage around the driver and a harness to hold the driver in the seat. Funny cars must also have an automatic fire extinguishing system and a safety hatch in the roof. The hatch allows the driver to exit a funny car quickly during an emergency.

Most drag strips are not long enough for cars to slow down gradually. Dragsters must stop quickly at the end of a race. Their braking systems may not be strong enough to stop them in time. Many dragsters use a parachute to stop. The driver releases the parachute from the rear of the vehicle after the race is over. It creates air resistance to quickly slow down the dragster.

A safety harness holds a driver tightly in the seat.

Chapter 2

Top Fuel Dragsters

Top fuel dragsters, or top fuelers, are the fastest class in drag racing. These long, narrow vehicles burn a fuel called nitromethane, or nitro. Top fuelers can travel up to 330 miles (531 kilometers) per hour. They can complete a quarter-mile race in about 4.5 seconds. During this time, they use about 15 gallons (57 liters) of fuel.

Creation of Top Fuel Dragsters

During the 1950s, drivers learned that cars with long, narrow designs were good for racing. Some drivers stripped the body panels from their cars to make them narrower. They

Top fuelers are the fastest drag racing vehicles.

Dragsters with long, narrow designs are often called rails.

called these cars "rails." With time, long, narrow body designs became more popular for drag racing. Today, top fuelers have this shape. Some people still call these dragsters rails.

Top fuelers do not burn gasoline as early dragsters did. In 1957, Emery Cook became the first driver to use nitromethane fuel. The nitro gave Cook's dragster a huge speed burst.

None of the other drivers could keep up with him.

The NHRA quickly banned nitro. Officials said it gave drivers an unfair advantage. Other racing organizations allowed drivers to use nitro. Nitro drag races became popular. NHRA officials were afraid that they would lose fans, so they allowed some dragster classes to use nitro.

Designing Top Fuel Dragsters

Today, top fuelers are the most popular type of dragsters. A top fueler's main frame, or chassis, is made of about 300 feet (91 meters) of lightweight chromoly tubes. These tubes are very strong, but they weigh only about 600 pounds (270 kilograms).

The outside body of a top fueler is made of aluminum and carbon fiber. This material is also used to build parts of some jet fighter planes. Nine main panels make up the body of a top fueler. Strong fasteners hold the panels together.

Dragsters have small front tires and large rear tires. The front tires are very narrow. They are used for steering. The rear tires are about 18 inches (46 centimeters) wide and about 3 feet (1 meter) in diameter. They are called slicks because they are completely smooth. Their smooth surface gives the tires good grip on paved tracks.

Top fuelers use supercharged engines called hemi engines. These engines are different from the engines in standard street cars. They do not burn fuel in tube-shaped head chambers as most car engines do. Instead, they burn nitro inside bowl-shaped chambers.

Top fueler engines have superchargers, which help the engines produce more than 6,000 horsepower. Standard street cars produce only about 150 horsepower. This extra power allows top fuelers to reach speeds of more than 330 miles (531 kilometers) per hour.

Dragsters have small front tires and large rear tires.

Chapter 3

Pro Stock Cars

Pro stock cars, or pro stockers, are based on standard car models. Racing teams modify these cars to make them light and streamlined. They also add very powerful engines. These changes allow pro stockers to reach speeds of more than 200 miles (322 kilometers) per hour.

Early Pro Stockers
The earliest drag racing vehicles were stock cars. Drivers bought standard cars and turned them into racing machines. As drag racing grew in popularity, many cars were built just for drag racing. But some drivers still enjoyed

Pro stockers are based on standard car models.

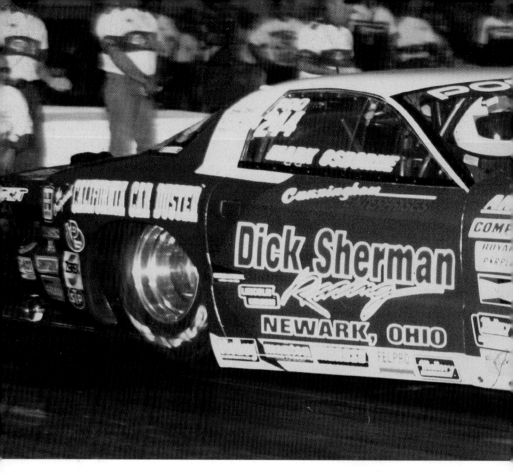

Pro stockers are powered by large V-8 engines.

racing standard cars. These drivers started the
pro stock class.

The most popular forms of stock car racing
are held on oval tracks. The National Association
for Stock Car Auto Racing (NASCAR) formed
in 1948 to organize this form of stock car

racing. Stock car racing became a popular
sport. The interest in NASCAR helped increase
fan interest in stock car drag racing as well.

Early pro stockers developed alongside
stock cars. In 1952, the Pure Oil company
made a new kind of slick tire just for stock
cars. Later, stock car race teams added roll

cages to protect drivers during crashes. They also made better suspension systems.

The biggest change to stock cars was the addition of powerful engines. In 1955, the Chevrolet company built a large, powerful V-8 engine. This type of eight-cylinder engine is still used in stock cars today.

Pro Stocker Design

Today, pro stockers are different from NASCAR stock cars. They are lighter and more powerful. They are built specially for very short races. Race teams carefully modify their cars to have the best possible acceleration.

Pro stockers in NHRA races must be based on a two-door car model from 1991 or later. Most of the car's parts, including headlights, taillights, and the manufacturer's logo, must be in their original position. Race teams must keep the original roof and rear body panels. The rest of the body is built from fiberglass or another strong, lightweight material. The

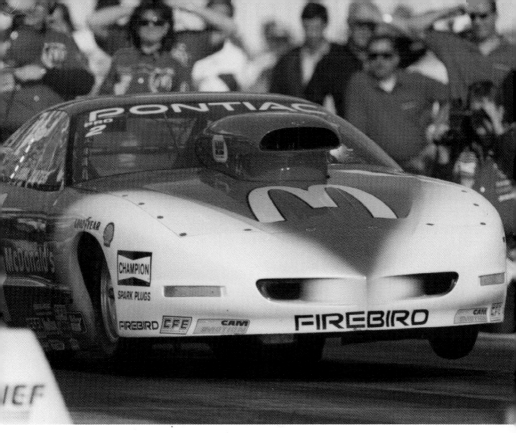

Race teams must keep many of a pro stocker's original parts.

body still looks like the original model, but it is much lighter.

A spoiler sits on the rear of the body. This winglike part is similar to the airfoil on top fuel dragsters. Air flowing over it creates downforce, which helps the rear tires grip the track.

Several types of engines are common in pro stockers. The most popular are the GM big-block wedge, the Chrysler B-1 wedge, and the Ford Boss 429-type hemi.

Pro stocker race teams are not allowed to use alcohol fuels, nitro, or superchargers. Instead, they use high-grade racing gasoline with an octane number of 118. The octane number measures the quality of gasoline. Standard cars use gasoline with an octane number between 87 and 93.

Pro stockers have large rear wheels and strong brakes. The rear wheels are usually about 17 inches (43 centimeters) wide. Four-wheel disk brakes help stop the car at the end of the race. Pro stockers sometimes use parachutes to stop as well.

Parachutes help pro stockers stop quickly.

Chapter 4

Nitro Funny Cars

Funny cars look like pro stockers on the outside. They have the basic shape of a standard car. Underneath the outside body, or shell, a funny car is more like a top fuel dragster than a pro stocker. Funny cars are built on a larger, stronger chassis. They also have powerful supercharged engines that burn nitro. This design allows funny cars to reach speeds of about 325 miles (523 kilometers) per hour.

Early Funny Cars

During the early and mid-1960s, top fuel dragsters and stock cars were the most popular

Funny cars have the basic shape of a standard car.

forms of drag racing cars. That fact changed in 1966, when racer Don Nicholson introduced the first flip-top drag racer. Nicholson built a car on a strong chassis. He gave it a powerful engine. He then built a one-piece shell that easily flipped up and down on top of the chassis.

Fans liked Nicholson's new car. Newspaper reporters wrote stories about it. They thought the car's design was funny, so they called it a "funny car."

Other drivers wanted to build their own funny cars. In 1968, Don Prudhomme built a funny car that he named Snake. The car won many races and was popular with fans.

Driver Tom McEwen was a friend of Prudhomme. McEwen built his own funny car and named it Mongoose. A mongoose is an animal that often eats dangerous snakes. McEwen and Prudhomme often raced their cars against each other. The cars became so

The outside body of a funny car is called the shell.

popular that the Mattel toy company paid them for the right to build toy models of their cars.

Early funny cars used only alcohol fuel. As funny car racing grew in popularity, many drivers used nitro and superchargers. Some of today's funny cars still use only alcohol fuel. But the fastest funny cars burn both alcohol fuel and nitro.

Funny Car Design

Today, an NHRA funny car's body must be based on a two-door car model made in 1991 or later. The outside shell is made of shaped carbon fiber. The shell weighs between 87 and 89 pounds (39.5 and 40.4 kilograms). Strong windows made of a material called Lexan fit into the shell. NHRA rules prevent funny cars from having built-in spoilers. But race teams can attach a spoiler to the rear of the shell. Teams also add parachutes to help slow down the cars.

A funny car's chassis is similar to that of a top fueler. It is made of chromoly tubes and weighs about 125 pounds (57 kilograms).

Most funny cars are powered by an aluminum 426 Chrysler hemi engine. Many of these engines include a supercharger.

Funny cars have large rear tires and small front tires. The rear tires are slicks. They are usually about 18 inches (46 centimeters) wide and about 3 feet (1 meter) in diameter. The

Strong windows made of a material called Lexan fit into a funny car's shell.

rear tires are not completely filled with air. This low air pressure allows more of the tire to grip the track, which improves the car's acceleration. The front tires are smaller. They are usually less than 2 feet (0.6 meters) in diameter.

Many of a funny car's design features are included for safety. All funny cars must have an escape hatch in the roof. This hatch allows the driver to get out quickly during an emergency. The car's side windows must have a 6-inch (15-centimeter) opening. This opening allows fire crews to put water hoses inside in case the car catches on fire.

Funny cars need parachutes to slow down after reaching speeds of 325 miles (523 kilometers) per hour.

Chapter 5

Other Drag Racing Vehicles

Top fuelers, pro stockers, and funny cars are the most popular drag racing classes today. But the NHRA organizes races for more than 200 classes of drag racing vehicles.

Top Alcohol Dragsters
Top alcohol dragsters are also called Federal-Mogul dragsters. They are similar to top fuel dragsters, but they do not use nitro fuel. Top alcohol dragsters burn an alcohol-based fuel called methanol.

Top alcohol dragsters are like top fuelers, but they do not use nitro.

They can reach speeds of about 270 miles (435 kilometers) per hour.

Top alcohol racing teams often work with smaller budgets than top fuel teams do. Their cars are often built in small private garages. The chassis and body of a top alcohol dragster are almost the same as those of top fuelers. Only the engines are different. Top alcohol dragsters use blown-alcohol engines. These engines are named for a part called a screw-blower, which shoots methanol fuel into the engine.

Motorcycle Drag Racing

Not all drag racing vehicles are cars. Several drag racing classes are for motorcycles. Pro stock bikes and pro modified bikes are two of the most popular motorcycle classes.

Like pro stock cars, pro stock bikes must be based on standard street models. NHRA bikes must be based on a model built in 1993 or later. The motorcycles must have their original headlights, taillights, and markings.

The NHRA holds many motorcycle drag races.

Pro modified bikes are also based on
standard motorcycles, but racing teams are
free to make more changes to the bikes. They
may add a completely new, lightweight body to
a motorcycle. They may also add larger, more
powerful engines.

39

Super stock vehicles are based on a particular model of car or truck.

Other Races

Drivers can take part in drag races for many other vehicles. Monster truck drag racing is popular in many areas. These large trucks have giant wheels that can easily drive over other cars.

Super stock drag races include many models of older vehicles. Super stock vehicles are similar to pro stockers. They are based on a particular model of a car or truck.

Large vehicles such as tractor trailers and limousines may take part in exhibition races. These races are not organized by the NHRA. They are held just for show. Drivers have added powerful engines from jet airplanes to some of these vehicles. This change makes the vehicles fast and dangerous. Most drivers choose to race in one of the main NHRA classes. Drivers know that they must stay safe so they can continue to enjoy their sport.

Words to Know

asphalt (ASS-fawlt)—a smooth, even pavement used on drag racing strips

chassis (CHASS-ee)—the frame on which the body of a car is built

chromoly (KROH-muh-lee)—a mixture of two metals called chromium and molybdenum

elimination (ee-lim-uh-NAY-shuhn)—a drag race between two cars

hemi (HEM-ee)—an engine that burns fuel in bowl-shaped chambers

methanol (METH-uh-nawl)—an alcohol-based fuel used by some dragsters

nitromethane (nye-troh-MEH-thane)—a mix of nitric acid and propane gas used as fuel in some dragsters

slicks (SLIKS)—soft tires that have no tread

To Learn More

Cook, Nick. *The World's Fastest Cars.* Built for Speed. Mankato, Minn.: Capstone Press, 2001.

Deady, Kathleen W. *Dragsters.* Wild Rides! Mankato, Minn.: Capstone Press, 2002.

Pitt, Matthew. *Drag Racer.* Built for Speed. New York: Children's Press, 2001.

Useful Addresses

**Canadian Motorcycle Drag
  Racing Association**
P.O. Box 93082
Langley, BC V3A 8H2
Canada

Museum of Drag Racing
13700 SW 16th Avenue
Ocala, FL 34473

National Hot Rod Association (NHRA)
2035 Financial Way
Glendora, CA 91741

Internet Sites

Do you want to learn more about dragsters?
Visit the FACT HOUND at *http://www.facthound.com*

FACT HOUND can track down many sites to help you.
All the FACT HOUND sites are hand-selected by Capstone
Press editors. FACT HOUND will fetch the best, most accurate
information to answer your questions.

IT IS EASY! IT IS FUN!
1) Go to *http://www.facthound.com*
2) Type in: 0736815007
3) Click on "FETCH IT" and FACT HOUND will put you on
the trail of several helpful links.

**You can also search by subject or book title. So, relax
and let our pal FACT HOUND do the research for you!**

Index